SINGLE MOM
MILLIONAIRE

By

Debbie Kempen

ISBN 979-8-9922396-0-7

your life forever. If you want to be financially independent, you need this book!

Alexis Smith

This book is made for all the "badass" women of the world. From the stories of true grit and determination to the lessons of money management, this book is sure to capture you and leave you inspired. A hidden gem waiting to be discovered is within your grasp.

Michael Prentice

Single Mom Millionaire is an inspiring and transformative read that every woman, especially single mothers navigating life after leaving abusive situations, should have on their shelf. The book expertly combines practical financial advice with deep empathy, offering step-by-step guidance on budgeting, building credit, saving, and investing, all tailored to the unique challenges women face. Its empowering tone motivates readers to take control of their financial futures, no matter their

WHAT PEOPLE SAY

Single Mom Millionaire is an inspiring read for all those single moms and women out there who suddenly find themselves back at the beginning in life. Single Mom Millionaire shows us it's never too late to turn your life around. Packed with plenty of practical advice this is a great read to get some clarity and guidance on your financial trajectory and perhaps reignite that fire we all have inside us!

Heidi De Love

Eye opening! Relatable and Relevant! This book inspired me to create tactics for my life's action plan.

Shelly Stienbarger

This book is a must for readers looking to start their personal finance and investment journey, especially for women and single mothers. The structure makes it easy to read without being overwhelming and the author inspires hope and motivation to take the steps that will change starting point. What truly stands out is its focus on rebuilding confidence and self-worth, proving that financial independence is not just about money but reclaiming one's power and freedom. This book is a lifeline for anyone ready to create a brighter, more secure future for themselves and their children.

Portia Runnels

Single Mom Millionaire shows astonishing will and power. It exemplifies how to change your current circumstances as a single mom, not only for yourself, but for your children that depend on you. This inspirational book will transport you to think of unconventional paths to achieve financial dreams and aspirations. A must read for women striving for knowledge in real estate and overcoming obstacles. Reading this book made me feel like I was talking to a friend, being given guidance.

Beatrice Gallo

COPYRIGHTS & LEGAL DISCLAIMER

nature or denomination on a par with as set out in this work.

Within "Single Mom Millionaire" the ideas and suggestions, even when describing an opinion of an expert or similar, offer their contribution for information purposes only. The content does not constitute professional, financial, legal, medical or psychological advice. It is at the free discretion of the reader of "Single Mom Millionaire" and its absolute responsibility for any willingness to follow or replicate some of the advice proposed there or to contact other competent personnel, according to their own beliefs, knowledge, habits and wills.

Everything included within "Single Mom Millionaire" must always be understood as the subjective opinion of the author, given that these considerations can also run counter to the precepts of knowledge taught in universities and / or in the financial or business world and therefore should be considered as simple expressions or controversies of a personal and in any case non-professional nature.

SINGLE MOM MILLIONAIRE

TABLE OF CONTENTS

DEDICATION

This book is dedicated to my children; Max, Arianna, and Alexia. You gave me the strength to keep pushing myself on the days I thought I couldn't.

Dear Reader,

If you feel behind your peers in milestones, career moves, or finances, I am here to tell you that you *can* catch up. Not only can you catch up, but you can exponentially surpass your peers. It all comes down to determination and education. Statistics may not be on your side, but you do not have to settle for these numbers. You have the power to rewrite your story, and your journey to success starts right here, right now.

Let us be the generation of women who change the outcome for our children.

If you want financial security and freedom, you must first change your mindset, followed by strategic action. The legacy we leave behind doesn't have to mirror the limitations of the past. You have the ability to break through barriers, and set a new standard of what's possible. If you want financial security and freedom, it starts with changing your mindset. When you believe that success is possible for you, everything else follows. You are capable of so much more than you realize, and this is your time to rise. I am here to guide you, support you, and cheer you on every step of the way. Together, we can create a new future, not just for ourselves, but for the next generation of women who will follow in our footsteps.

Letter to the Single Mom:

You are amazing. The fact that you're holding this book in your hands right now shows your commitment to yourself and your future. It shows that you're ready to step into your power, to create the life you've always dreamed of for yourself and your children, no matter where you are on your journey.

As a single mom myself, I understand the challenges you face — the sleepless nights, the juggling act between work, parenting, and everything in between. It's hard, but let me remind you of something powerful: You are stronger than you think. You have a resilience inside of you that is untouchable. The love and dedication you pour into your family is immeasurable, and that same energy is what will propel you forward as you build the wealth and financial freedom you deserve.

This book isn't just a guide to financial success — it's a message of empowerment. It's proof that no matter where you start, no matter how many obstacles you face, you can rise. I've been there, I know how it feels to feel overwhelmed, underprepared, or like the odds are stacked against you. But trust me, you have the ability to transform your life. You are capable of more than you realize, and you don't have to do it alone.

In these pages, you'll find not just strategies for investing, but stories of strength, resilience, and hope. My journey wasn't easy, but it was worth it. And if I can do it, so can you. You don't have to wait for the "perfect moment" or for things to fall into place. The moment is now, and you have everything you need to begin this new chapter. Keep going, keep pushing, and know that every step you take brings you closer to the life you're meant to live.

FOREWORD

I can't tell you how happy I am to see everything that my mom has accomplished. She is my biggest role model, and I really look up to her. She taught me that anything is possible with a disciplined mindset and clear goals. I'm so proud of her every day, and it makes me appreciate having gotten to grow up with her.

Alexia

Chapter 1: How It Started

"The more vulnerable you are talking about money, the more likely you are to attract like-minded people."

Debbie Kempen

I vividly remember the day I escaped my ex-husband, three babies in tow. I looked back at our home on my way out the door and made a very powerful promise to myself. This promise was, "When I am on my feet, I will help other women escape situations like this. Women who feel like they can't afford to leave because they don't have the means to support themselves".

This book is the first step in making that promise a reality, and I am so thankful you are a part of this journey.

I hope this book will inspire you to never settle for less, regardless of your current circumstances. There is success on the other side!

Now let me tell you how my story began...so you understand what I mean when I say, "If I can do it, anyone can." I was 19 when I agreed to get married. To be honest, I had a moment of doubt, but I didn't want to hurt his feelings. He had been my friend for the last 1 ½ years. Can you believe I made a life-changing decision, like getting married, because I didn't want to hurt his feelings? I was raised to be the good girl. The keep quiet and follow directions girl.

I was pregnant shortly after, and six weeks after that he deployed. It was your common pre-deployment story. He was gone for 18 months and came home when our baby girl was 8 months old. He came back in body but not in spirit. This was the beginning of the end of our marriage. It was tumultuous, to say the least. We rode it out for 10 solid years.

In those ten years I endured physical, emotional, verbal and financial abuse. Nothing "we" owned was mine. Every time I tried to leave the house to get the kids away from him punching holes into the wall and yelling, I was met with him yanking the keys, the stroller, and our jackets from us. Every time he said, "You can't leave...that car is mine! That stroller? I paid for that! Those jackets are mine."

I did not spend money on myself, while he splurged on hunting and fishing gear. He bought a new vehicle every six months. By the end of our marriage he was withdrawing $2000 per month in cash. Meanwhile, my debit card was getting declined for milk at the grocery store. I had to ask him a question no wife should ever have to ask her husband, "Are you supporting another family?" His answer was obviously, "No." At this point I'm left to assume he was either spending it on drugs or hiding it because he knew the inevitable was coming. I had just resumed taking college courses.

He said to me,"I know what you're doing."

I asked,"What?"

He said,"You're finishing your degree so you can leave me."

My answer was clearly, "No."

The reality is that I was absolutely planning my exit from this marriage. I was scared of what he would do if I told him this. His drug and alcohol addiction had become dangerous to me and the kids. His mental health was on a quick decline.

The big finale. That's how I refer to the last day we lived in our home together. It was the worst combination of all forms of abuse. I won't get into too much detail because that's not what this book is about. I will say it ended it with death threats. No woman should be afraid for her life in her own home, the home she is raising her children in.

This was the day I started the long journey of healing. I knew I was not going to live my life as a victim. I knew I needed to recover from this to make sure my daughters don't make the same mistakes I did. I knew I wasn't alone in the mistakes I made that got me here. According to the Domestic Violence Hotline (www.thehotline.org) 1 in 4 women in the U.S. have experienced severe physical violence by an intimate partner in their lifetime. Keep in mind that this statistic is based on reported cases. Many cases go unreported; it's estimated that only 34% of people injured by intimate partners receive medical care for their injuries. In cases of homicide where women are the victims, more than half are killed by current or former intimate partners.

After my escape, I filed, and was granted a long-term protective order against him for myself and the kids. In those first six months I felt so much regret. I reflected on every red flag that I ignored. I thought over and over again, "I should have left him when he did this or that." My reality was that I didn't and now I'm a single mom of three young kids- 3 ,4, and 8 years old.

Along with the regret came shame and a feeling of being undeserving. I moved into a house close to my parents to make childcare easier. It was a family neighborhood. I felt like I did not deserve to be there. This feeling was validated when the neighbor's daughter came over one day to ask if my kids could play. I said yes and before the kids left the house I gave them a kiss. This little five year-old girl looked at me and said, "You're allowed to kiss your kids because you don't have a husband."

How do you recover from having your whole future as you saw it ripped from you? I went from being a stay at home mom for ten years and having a shared dream with my husband of owning a hobby farm with white picket fence to suddenly working 12 hour shifts, struggling to pay rent. At the time I just went into survival mode. I started running and found it therapeutic. It was a way to clear my mind. Once I was able to do that I could slowly start to make new dreams for myself. I cannot change the outcome of the decisions I made in the past. I can only learn from them and keep going. I can create new goals and a new life.

When it comes to changing the projected outcome of the path you are on, two key factors play a crucial role: gaining knowledge and taking action. You have taken the first step already! One thing to be mindful of is spending too much time in the education part of it. I see too many people diving deep into learning and education and never taking action. It is in the actions that you take that will change the outcome of your future. When it comes to making your money grow and work for you, time is your friend. The sooner you take action, the longer your money sits in that investment and the sooner you can create abundance for you and your family. Stop working so hard for money and make your money work for you. This book will provide you with everything you need to know to get started in investing in real estate. You can find more resources and support by visiting my website at www.debbiekempen.com.

You have likely never had conversations around money and wealth with your family or friends, or at least not the right ones. You likely never learned about money and investing in school, yet it is the single most important, life-changing thing that you can learn, aside from maintaining your physical health. Talking about money has become so taboo in our culture. It seems to me there are two fears that come up in conversations about money. It's either 1) I don't have enough of it and people will judge me, or 2) I have a lot of it and people will try to take it from me. Neither of these are true if you are in healthy relationships with the people you surround yourself with. In fact, the more vulnerable you are talking about money, the more likely you are to attract like-minded people. These people and conversations will later help you speed up your way to wealth and prosperity.

"*Money is the last taboo. People will talk about their sex lives before they talk about their finances*"
Marvin H. Mcintyre

Let's talk about money. I grew up in a lower-middle class family to parents who grew up extremely poor. Our status as a lower-middle class family often dipped below that, to poor. Do you remember that funny line in Meet the Fockers when Bernie Focker says, "If it's yellow let it mellow, if it's brown flush it down."? My family actually did that. We had times in our childhood where everything we owned came to us as donations from friends and family, or the dump. Yes, that's right. I had a dresser that was acquired at the dump, and yes, it did smell funny. Money and wealth are not always a progressive line on a chart. Sometimes it fluctuates and that's ok.

Most of our parents grew up in a world where money was scarce. *Their* parents survived the Great Depression and WWII, so it is no surprise that our parents were not taught anything about money other than "save, save, save!" My dad was raised by a single mother who bounced from house to house because she couldn't afford rent. My mother grew up in a post-WWII economy in Germany. Needless to say, I grew up in a home where it was NOT ok to spend money on anything that you didn't absolutely need. As the third kid out of four, I knew not to ask for anything.

My dad decided in his 40's that he wanted to change the outcome of his family's wealth. He stumbled across the book "Rich Dad Poor Dad" by Robert Kiyosaki. I was a teenager when he started to invest in real estate. He started with small homes, rented them out and eventually sold them to upgrade to duplex, triplexes and 4-plexes. Those 4plexes have since then been upgraded to 12 unit apartment buildings. He is my "rags-to-riches" inspiration. He proves that regardless of your past, your age, or your current circumstances you can create generational wealth for your family. He continued to live frugally despite growing his real estate portfolio. I've been telling him for years that he has done such a good job raising us, that we have gone on to build our own wealth. He can release the pressure of leaving behind a monetary legacy and enjoy life. He is finally rewiring his brain to enjoy the fruits of his labor.

I graduated Highschool with more education in finances than most. I am thankful for that. It is one of the reasons I am so passionate about educating others on finances and investing. It does not go to say that I did not have my own obstacles to overcome. My obstacles were different from those of my parents and I have developed my own approach to building wealth and how to enjoy it. These are specific to women and life as a single mother.

As I started reading personal development books, specifically those about money, business, investing and real estate I began to evolve my views on money. As a busy single mother with a very distracted mind, I have found that listening to the audio version in my car is the most effective way for me to absorb them. I started noticing however, that the books that were written and narrated by men were making me tired. One of them was so bad that I couldn't listen to it in the car anymore. I even started listening to it at night when I couldn't sleep. It worked like a charm! That was when I realized there aren't enough money books written by women FOR women.

I am no stranger to male-dominated spaces. I am serving in the Air National Guard and my hobbies consist of traditionally male things, like weightlifting. Men have a way of exuding confidence in areas they know little about. When the topic of money comes up, I have a lot to say. I have been called a slumlord by many men in their mid 40s because they are intimidated by my success. How dare a woman who is a single-mother and a lower-ranking airman make more money than them!

I have given men real estate investing advice just to have them disregard me. The next day that same man will say he's ready to buy a house because so-and-so, a man, explained to him the benefits of owning a home vs renting. The man gave him the SAME advice! Why didn't it land when I told him to do it? I was offended at first, but the reality is, that we are more likely to process the advice given to us if it is coming from someone who is relatable. If you read a book written by a multi-millionaire who came from a wealthy family, you are less likely to execute the tactics being taught because you know he had a head start on his success, whereas you did not.

I am a single mother who went through a really nasty divorce. I may have had an advantage in the early stages of my adult life, but the ramifications of my divorce took me down. My divorce cost me over 70 thousand dollars in legal fees, and took 1 ½ years to finalize. In that time, the investment properties I owned with my ex-husband went into foreclosure. It took them another 1 ½ years for the bank to finalize the foreclosure. If you understand credit reports, that means that my credit report showed delinquencies for 1 ½ years, and the foreclosures didn't show up on my credit report for another 1 ½ years. The clock doesn't start on your foreclosure until it is finalized. Negative inquiries on your credit report fall off after 7 years. That means it will take 10 years for my credit report to recover from this divorce. It is through this struggle, that I got creative and learned how to invest in real estate without using my credit score.

I was angry. I was thirty years old and spent ten years as a stay-at-home mom. I did not have a career. I did not have a retirement account. My credit report was shit. My ex-husband quit his job so he wouldn't have to pay child support. How do you recover from that? My whole life plans were gone. What do you do when you plan your entire future with someone for ten years and then suddenly it's gone? What man is going to love me now that I am a single mom of three young kids?

As simple as it sounds, the phrase that got me through the hardest times was, "It is what it is". There are things that happen in divorce that we cannot control, no matter how much we wish we could. Whether it's the actions of your ex, the legal system, or the emotional toll, there are factors beyond your influence. But here's the powerful truth: the sooner you stop fighting what's out of your hands, the sooner you'll find peace. Letting go doesn't mean giving up — it means accepting reality and focusing on what you *can* change. Once you release what you can't control, you can start working towards solutions. Accepting what "is" doesn't limit you; it frees you. That's when true progress begins.

> "Perhaps the butterfly is proof that you can go through a great deal of darkness yet become something beautiful"

Chapter 2: Mind Over Matter

"If you change the way you look at things, the things you look at change"

Wayne Dyer

Nothing in your life will change if you don't change your mindset. Up until now you've been told to go to school, get good grades, and go to college. If you didn't go to college you were made to feel like you wouldn't be successful. If you did go to college you were left with thousands of dollars of debt upon graduating.

It has been drilled into our minds that we need to find a good paying job that offers a retirement plan, 401k, and medical insurance. If you're lucky you might get two weeks of paid time off and holidays with your family. In today's economy most Americans are working overtime or more than one job, and let's face it, most of us don't even like our jobs.

In Bronnie Ware's book, "The Five Regrets of the Dying", she describes the personal growth and emotions of those who are near the end of their lives. She asked them if they had any regrets or if there was anything they would do differently. The most common responses were as follows:

1) I wish I had the courage to live a life true to myself, not the life others expected of me.
2) I wish I hadn't worked so hard.
3) I wish I had the courage to express my feelings.
4) I wish I had stayed in touch with my friends.
5) I wish I had let myself be happier.

After I filed for divorce, I started working a job I knew I wouldn't love. It was the best paying job I could get at the time. I am thankful to have had that job to jump into right away. I am thankful that I was able to support myself and three kids by myself with that income, but it was not fulfilling. After the first year, the hours, night shifts and windowless days started getting to me. I decided to come up with an exit strategy.

I knew I wanted to have a schedule that was more accommodating to the life of a single mom. I was already passionate about investing in real estate, so I decided to get my real estate license. I continued to work the other job until I was able to pay off my lawyer ($70.000) and my $50,000 car. I did not want to start this new chapter with debt, or to feel any type of financial stress. I started talking about my plan to other people and learned a very important lesson from that. People will always try to talk you out of a plan that doesn't line up with what they're doing, so be 100% determined to follow through with your plan before you share it with other people. They will, without a doubt, try to talk you out of it. Understandably, I'd be upset too if I had spent twenty years doing something I hate just because society told me to.

I reached my goal with a sense of urgency! Like my life depended on it, because it truly felt like it did! I knew I was going to have the courage to live a life true to myself, not the life others expected of me NOW. I made a promise to myself that I will not live a life of regret. I will do what feels right to me. I will *trust* myself to make good decisions for myself and my three children. Learning to trust yourself is so important in this journey! We learn to trust ourselves by setting goals, reaching those goals, and then doing it again. The crazier the goal you accomplish, the faster you learn to trust yourself. I've gotten to the point where I probably just sound crazy to other people. I still hear people say "that's an unrealistic goal". To that I say, "WATCH ME!"

I get it. We need to feed our families, but it's time to view your job as a tool to get you to where you want to be and not the MEANS to get you where you want to be. Working your 9-5 pays the bills and gets you by. You might even have that lucrative 401k, however, it will not generate long-term wealth for you and your family. It's up to you to learn and DO the things that will give you a comfortable retirement, and maybe even allow you to retire early.

Living with the idea that money is scarce impacts your daily actions in such a way that prohibits growth. If I had felt like money is scarce, I never would have made risky, yet rewarding, investment decisions. If I felt money was scarce, I would not have moved to Germany and traveled the world for unpaid modeling gigs, which are now part of my extensive branding portfolio. (It was actually cheaper than paying a branding photographer in the US). If I felt like money was scarce I would stay home out of fear of spending money, but instead I am networking with the right people to propel me forward and bouncing ideas off of other successful people.

When we operate from a place of fear or scarcity, we tend to repel financial opportunities by unconsciously reinforcing the belief that we lack resources. In contrast, gratitude and abundance-focused thinking project a positive energy that draws others toward collaboration, generosity, and shared success. By becoming aware of these emotional influences, individuals can consciously align their financial actions with the energy they wish to attract. Techniques like mindfulness, journaling, or even gratitude practices can help shift emotions toward a more empowered financial state.

Rewiring your brain to allow abundance and joy in your life takes time. It means constantly reminding yourself of what your long-term plan is throughout your daily actions. Be aware of the thoughts that come to mind in different money situations. When you have a negative feeling around money, reword those thoughts into something more positive. I used to struggle with letting money go. Any trip to the grocery store that ended in spending over $100 gave me a small panic attack- and that's pretty much every time when you have kids. I *hated* going grocery shopping! I had to rewire my brain around spending money. I started reminding myself of what I was doing when I was spending money on necessary items, like groceries, utilities and clothing for my children. "I am thankful that I have the means to provide food and clothing for my three children." When I'm shocked by a high utility bill I say, "I am thankful to have power and electricity". I will include some money affirmations at the end of this chapter.

When you start to view success as a game, everything starts to make more sense. Like any game, there are rules, strategies, and even a few loopholes. Whether you like it or not, everyone is playing this game, and ignoring the rules won't stop the game from happening — it just leaves you, and your family at a disadvantage. Success is about engaging, learning how the game works, and positioning yourself to win. Educating yourself means learning from others who have already won, and using them to your benefit — it's about being savvy, resourceful, and proactive.

Up until now, your perception of people with money has likely been shaped by negative examples. We see reality stars, influencers, and celebrities with no apparent talents making billions just by exposing their families and creating fake drama for the media. We hear about corrupt CEOs and politicians making unethical decisions that harm millions of people, all for their own financial gain. Stories of greed, power, and even violence for the sake of success, fame, and fortune dominate the news. It's easy to associate wealth with negativity when so many of the people in the spotlight seem to represent the worst of human behavior.

But what if we shifted our perspective? What if more good people had money—people like you, who care about others and want to make a positive impact? Imagine the change that could happen if more individuals with integrity and compassion had the resources to shape the world. Money is simply a tool; in the hands of the right people, it can be used for incredible good. It can fund community projects, support causes that align with your values, create opportunities for others, and build legacies that lift people up instead of tearing them down.

In September of 2024, Hurricane Helene caused catastrophic damage to the southeast of the United States, killing hundreds of people and leaving thousands without power, and drinkable water. The government did little to provide immediate relief. Do you know who *did* help? A woman with wealth! Dolly Parton donated one million dollars of her own money and another million from her business to help the victims of Hurricane Helen. Dolly Parton has a long track record of doing good things with the money she makes. She is the founder of Imagination Library, which sends millions of books directly to children's homes. My family has been a recipient of this program and are very thankful for it. Some of our favorite books came from her.

What if instead of shying away from the pursuit of financial success, we embraced it with the intention of doing better- of being the change we wish to see? Having expendable income gives you freedom, influence, and the ability to make a difference. What would happen if more women had the financial means to create real, lasting change in their communities? The possibilities are endless. It's time to rethink your relationship with money and see it as a force for good, one that can amplify your ability to live a life of purpose and service, rather than corruption and greed. The world needs more good people in positions of financial power — why not you?

What would you do with a million dollars? Imagine you already have everything you desire, want and need and you have an extra million dollars. Would you help out struggling family members? Would you donate to a cause that you're passionate about? There is so much good that we can do with money! The world needs more good people to be rich. In fact, we need more women to be rich! Women have proven time and time again to be better investors. Women are more likely to do good with excess money. According to the Women's Philanthropy Institute, women in the top 25% of wealth holders give 156% more to charity than men. It's not just the top 25% - women who are head of household, are more likely to give, regardless of their income level.

Money is everywhere, constantly flowing through our lives and the world around us. It circulates like energy, exchanged daily in businesses, transactions, and investments. Whether it's a few dollars or a million, money moves in abundance, always changing hands.

Money isn't scarce, it's not something only a few people can access. It's constantly replenishing and growing, available to anyone who wants it.

The belief that money is limited will hold you back. Money is available to you for the taking. Just as it moves easily from one person to the next, it can come to you too. The key is shifting your mindset—recognizing that money is not running out. It's a resource you can attract and use to build the life you desire. When you align yourself with this flow, opportunities to earn and grow wealth start to appear. Money, after all, is meant to circulate, and it can flow to you as easily as it does to anyone else.

Wanting more money than you need isn't selfish. It's ok to want more. Wanting money doesn't mean you're a greedy person. Having more money will give you freedom. Freedom to work when you want to work, not because the bills are due. The freedom to spend time with your family when they need you most. The ability to give back to people in need. The power to do what you want to help others.

No conversation about money mindset would be complete without bringing up money manifestation. Manifestation is not as simple as just dreaming your goals into existence. It is the process of bringing a goal, desire, or vision into reality by aligning your thoughts, emotions, and actions with the outcome you want to achieve. It often involves focusing on positive intentions, visualizing success, and taking purposeful steps toward your goals. Manifestation combines belief and effort, relying on the idea that your mindset and energy can influence the opportunities and results you attract in life. It's about creating a clear intention and following through with aligned actions to bring that intention to fruition.

To align yourself with receiving money, you need to cultivate a mindset of abundance and self-worth. Start by releasing limiting beliefs, like the idea that wealth is only for others or that you don't deserve financial success. Let go of thoughts like "I'm not good with money" or "I'll never get ahead"—they just block opportunities. Gratitude for your current resources is key. It shifts your energy toward positivity. Visualize your financial goals vividly, affirm your ability to create wealth, and take actionable steps toward them. Surround yourself with supportive influences, and stay open to opportunities, creating harmony between your thoughts, emotions, and actions to attract abundance. To try some free mindset mediations visit www.debbiekempen.com.

Your internal dialogue about money matters. As promised, let's talk about affirmations. Using affirmations daily is a powerful way to reprogram your mindset for success and abundance. Start each morning by repeating your affirmations out loud, in front of a mirror, writing them down in a journal, or putting them on post-it notes around the house. As you go about your day, keep these affirmations at the forefront of your mind, and whenever doubt or negative thoughts come to mind, replace them with your positive affirmations. By consistently focusing on these empowering statements, you'll start to shift your beliefs and attract the opportunities, wealth, and success you desire.

Here's a list of 20 powerful money mindset affirmations to empower you to build a strong, positive relationship with money:

- I deserve financial abundance, and I am open to receiving it.
- I am the creator of my own wealth and financial freedom.

- Money flows to me with ease, and I manage it wisely.
- I release any fear or doubt around money and embrace prosperity.
- I am in control of my financial future, and I make smart money decisions.
- I attract wealth through my skills, talents, and hard work.
- My financial success benefits myself and those around me.
- I am worthy of making more money than I ever imagined.
- I am a money magnet, and opportunities for wealth find me easily.
- I welcome financial freedom and the power to create the life I want.
- I have everything I need to achieve financial success.
- I am confident in my ability to attract wealth and abundance.
- My bank account grows every day, and I am grateful for my prosperity.
- I choose to focus on abundance rather than scarcity.
- I love money, and money loves me.
- I attract the right people and opportunities to grow my wealth.

- I use my wealth to create positive change in my life and the lives of others.
- I am aligned with the energy of wealth and abundance.
- Every dollar I spend comes back to me multiplied.
    - I am financially free, and I choose to live a life of wealth and abundance.

> *Living with the idea that money is scarce impacts your daily actions in such a way that prohibits growth.*
>
> Debbie Kempen

Chapter 3: Money Energy

"Money is a reflection of the energy you put into the world through your time, effort, and decisions."

Debbie Kempen

To solidify the importance of speaking positively to yourself and about yourself, let's talk about energy. Our bodies are made up of cells, cells are made of molecules, molecules are made of atoms, atoms are made of subatomic particles, and subatomic particles are energy. We are thus created from energy- an energy that can be altered by our surroundings and environment.

There is scientific evidence showing that how we think affects our physical being. Sixty percent of the human body is made up of water.

In 1994, Dr Masaru Emoto began researching how human consciousness affects the molecular structure of water. His book, The Hidden Messages in Water, was published in 2004. In his book he shares images of how conscious thoughts, words and prayer affect the appearance of the water molecules.

Using Magnetic Resonance Analysis technology and high-speed photographs, Dr. Emoto demonstrated how water exposed to loving, and compassionate human intention creates beautiful molecular formations in the water. On the contrary, water that was exposed to fearful, mean or displeasing words resulted in disconnected, disfigured and unpleasant physical molecular formations.

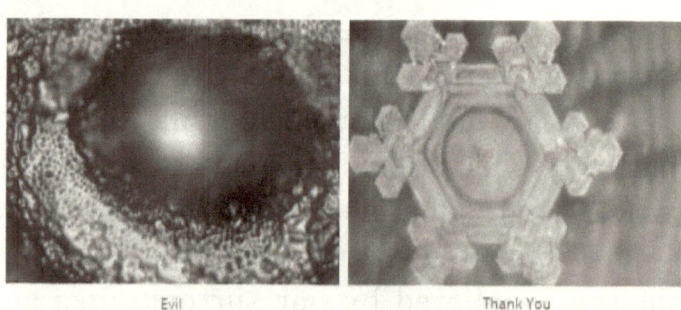

Evil   Thank You

Emoto, Masaru. *The Hidden Messages in Water*. Atria Books, 2005

The energy we carry within us does more than define our internal state—it radiates outward and influences the world around us.

Think about how someone's presence can shift the energy in a room, whether by bringing a sense of calm or tension. This demonstrates the power of our energy to shape interactions, opportunities, and even outcomes.

To empower yourself, start by being mindful of the energy you nurture within. Pay attention to how you speak to yourself and the feelings you dwell on. Negative self-talk and dwelling on scarcity can create a cycle that limits what you believe is possible. Instead, consciously create positive energy by focusing on gratitude. Reflect on the people, experiences, and resources in your life that bring joy or growth. A daily gratitude practice can be transformative, fostering a mindset of abundance rather than lack.

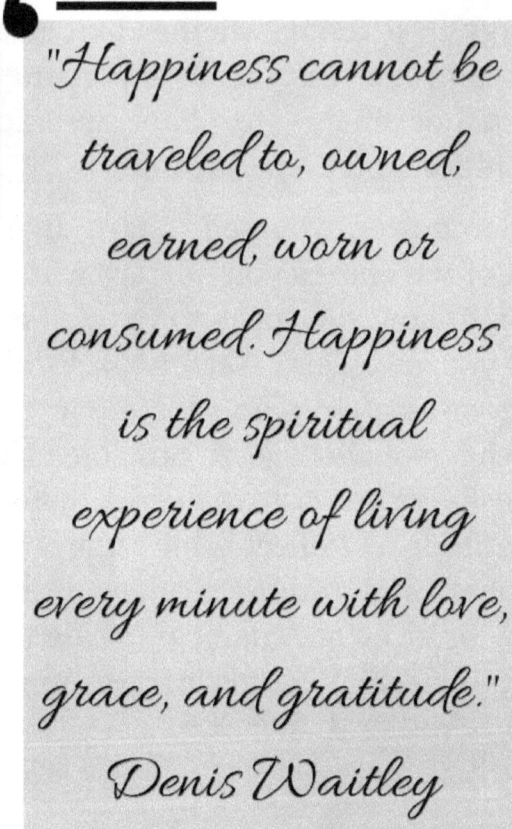

"Happiness cannot be traveled to, owned, earned, worn or consumed. Happiness is the spiritual experience of living every minute with love, grace, and gratitude."

Denis Waitley

As your internal energy becomes more positive, you'll naturally attract like-minded individuals. Surrounding yourself with others who seek the good in life amplifies your own capacity to see and seize opportunities. These connections can spark new ideas, provide encouragement, and expand your vision of what's possible. By cultivating a positive outlook and seeking out uplifting relationships, you position yourself not just to react to life, but to actively create a life of abundance and purpose.

This practice isn't just about feeling good — it's about aligning your energy with the life you want to build. Positive energy is a catalyst for progress and an open invitation to the opportunities waiting for you.

I decided to try a little experiment at work one day to test how much energy influences a space. I intentionally walked around the office with an upbeat, positive attitude, asking everyone how they were doing. At first, people were skeptical; after all, not many were genuinely thrilled to be at work. But as the day went on, something fascinating happened—my energy began to shift the atmosphere. I noticed everyone was a little bit happier. By the afternoon, a colleague came up to me and said, "It feels like everyone's in a better mood today. Your energy really rubbed off!"

This simple experiment reinforced a powerful truth: the energy we bring into a space shapes not only our own experience but also the experiences of those around us. It has a ripple effect. Positive energy has the ability to lift others, improve relationships, and even transform environments.

Think about the impact of this ripple effect on a larger scale. The energy you project doesn't just shape your day—it shapes your future. By consciously putting positivity into the world, you're not only creating a better experience for yourself but also opening doors to deeper connections, greater opportunities, and a brighter life. The next time you're in a challenging situation, remember this: your energy is a choice. Make it a conscious one, and watch as the universe reflects that positivity back to you.

Money isn't just a number in your bank account, it's a reflection of energy. Think of it as a manifestation of the energy you put into the world through your time, effort, and decisions. The definition of energy is to move, and just like energy, money is meant to keep moving. It's in constant motion, flowing from one person to another, creating opportunities, fostering growth, and building connections. When money stagnates, it loses its power. If you let money sit idle in your bank account, it won't be able to keep up with inflation, and over time, its value diminishes.

Money is meant to circulate, to change hands, to fuel new projects, ideas, and ventures. Just as energy flows and moves through all things, money should be treated the same way. It thrives when it's actively in motion, bringing value and receiving value in return. The key is not to hoard it, but to allow it to flow, knowing that every dollar spent or invested is an opportunity for new energy to enter your life.

Where you place your money is just as important as how you use it. It needs to be in vibration with your energy. In other words, the way you feel about money, your beliefs around it, and the actions you take, all align with the energy you're putting into the world. If you feel abundant and confident in your financial decisions, that energy will attract opportunities and wealth. When your mindset is aligned with abundance, the universe responds by bringing more of what you're vibrating out into the world.

By aligning your thoughts, emotions, and actions with the frequency of abundance, you begin to attract wealth. It's the universal law of attraction in action: like attracts like. If you believe you deserve wealth, if you act with confidence and integrity in your financial choices, and if you invest in yourself and in ventures that align with your values, you'll create a magnetic force for prosperity.

If you need more science-based evidence, I encourage you to look into the work of Dr. Joe Dispenza. He is a neuroscientist and author known for his work on how thoughts can shape our reality. He teaches that by consciously changing our thoughts and beliefs, we can rewire our brains and create lasting transformation. He emphasizes that thoughts generate electrical impulses in the brain, which affect our physical state and emotions. Through practices like meditation, individuals can reprogram their subconscious mind to remove limiting beliefs and align with positive outcomes. His work shows how harnessing the power of the mind can shift our energy and attract wealth, health, and success.

You have infinite potential. The money you need is already available to you. It's just waiting for you to align with the energy of abundance. The universe is abundant, and when you start vibrating at the frequency of prosperity, everything you need will flow to you. The key is to act from a place of abundance, to see opportunities where others see obstacles, and to trust that the more you give and receive, the more you'll attract.

Chapter 4: How to Save Money

Most people assume that saving money means to live a restrictive lifestyle. That means no more going out with friends, no more traveling, and telling your kids "no" when they ask for something. That sounds miserable. I'm not suggesting that you continue spending frivolously if you are in deep debt either, but there is a happy medium. I find that being too frugal is not sustainable for most of us.

If you are someone who historically spends too much money, it is time to evaluate why. If you are so frugal that you're not enjoying life, it's also time to evaluate why. There is a whole career field dedicated to the psychology of money. Use the affirmations I provided to you and do the exercises recommended in this book and do the necessary inner healing. These things need to be addressed as you continue your journey to wealth.

SINGLE MOM MILLIONAIRE

To save more or to make more, that is the question. Why not do both? Most of us have areas in our lives where we can easily cut back on expenses. When was the last time you checked those subscriptions on your phone from the app store? When was the last time you looked through your bank and credit card statements? I still find monthly charges that should have been cancelled a long time ago for products or services I no longer use. Chances are, you will too.

One of my favorite tactics for saving money is to have two separate bank accounts for different expenses. When I was paying off my debt like my life depended on it, I had one bank account for all my important monthly, recurring expenses. These were the ones I could not avoid paying. These included: rent, electricity, water, gas, car payment, and monthly minimum credit card payments. Then I gave myself a dollar amount that I was ok with spending on variable expenses. These are the expenses I have the most control over. It's how much money I'm spending on groceries every week. It's filling up my car with gas. I transferred that dollar amount into my "spending" account and did not let myself spend more than what I had in that account.

I moved closer to my parents during this time to make my life easier. It shortened my commute to work, and significantly reduced my grocery bill. Childcare was the biggest factor, however, mostly because there weren't any daycares open during the hours I needed them most. My parents were pivotal during this time in my life. I realize not everyone has this luxury. If you do not have supportive parents to lean on I suggest finding someone else in your life who you can trust to help out. Afterall, it takes a village to raise children. It's important for your kids to see that you are loved and supported by others.

During this time, I was also figuring out how to *make* more money. I understood and loved real estate investing so I got licensed to sell real estate. On my days off I was doing showings for other agents, and actively looking for my own clients. I was able to kill two birds with one stone by finding real estate clients at my primary job. Some of my coworkers were annoyed by my constant conversations about real estate but I generated so many clients out of it!

The brokerage I was licensed with was offering a sales class for $800. I was asked to participate, but I didn't have an extra $800 to spend on this. I was too determined to pay off my debts so I could quit my job! I was told over and over again that this class was well worth the $800 and that I would make that money back in new sales. I finally took the bait and signed up, and my God was this course life changing! It was not just a sales class. This was a personal development class. It was the personal development class I didn't know I needed. It was the first time in my life that I invested in *myself*. I share this with you to say, it is always worth it to invest in yourself. Saving money is not always the answer. You might miss out on powerful, life changing opportunities if you're too frugal.

This personal development class was like a gateway drug! Between two jobs, one of them shift work, I didn't have a ton of free time to go to classes or read books, so I started to listen to personal development books on audio. I signed up for a monthly subscription to buy one audio book per month. I often listen to the same book 2-3 times. Similar to daily affirmations, I found that listening to books about abundance, wealth, and success helped me keep me in a positive mindset about money and life in general. They still do to this day.

Invest in yourself! It doesn't need to be an $800 class, or a coaching program. It can be a $15/month subscription to audio books. We live in an era where we have easy access to resources. Take advantage of it! We have it easier than ever.

Investing in yourself doesn't just mean education. Investing in yourself can also mean spending money on that gym membership because you know that when you're working out you have better mental clarity, focus, energy and confidence. Investing in yourself can mean going to the hair salon and getting highlights, because you know it will help you put your best foot forward to accomplish your goals. It's important to find balance when setting financial goals. If you make yourself miserable, you'll burn out and the creative energy won't be available for you to tap in to.

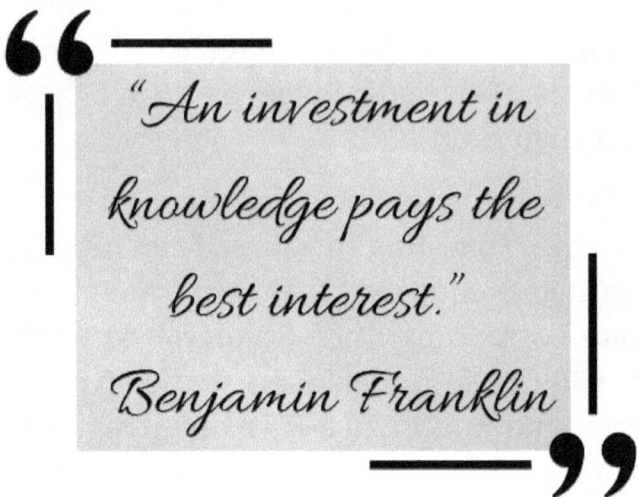

"*An investment in knowledge pays the best interest.*"
Benjamin Franklin

I recently heard a story where someone asked a group of entrepreneurs if they felt like they could make $1million in the next year. They all laughed and said no, it would take years to build up to that kind of revenue. Then the question was reworded, and they were asked if they could make $1million in a year if their families' lives depended on it. They all quickly responded that they would find a way to make $1million dollars if their families lives depended on it. It is a reminder that if we really put our mind to it, we will find a way. Don't put too many restrictions on your life or you'll close your mind to opportunities.

Exercise: I want you to get out a sheet of paper and write down 100 ways you could make money today- like you and your family's lives depended on it. Like your dog's life depends on it. Do not get up until you've written down 100 ideas. You might surprise yourself with how creative you get.

Here are some prompts to help spark ideas for making money:

- What skills or talents do you have that others might need or value?

Think about what you're good at, whether it's writing, design, organization, or teaching.

- What hobbies or activities do you enjoy that could be turned into a side business?

  Consider things you love doing, like crafting, cooking, photography, or fitness.

- Are there any services or products that people in your community or network frequently ask for?

  Identify a demand that you can meet.

- What problems do you see around you that you could solve?

  Consider common issues people face that you have a solution for.

- Is there a need for personal assistance or support in your area?

  From virtual assistance to pet-sitting, there are endless possibilities for service-based income.

- What are people willing to pay for that you can create or offer online?

Digital products like courses, e-books, or templates are low-cost to produce and can bring in passive income.

- Have you considered monetizing your knowledge?

  You can create a class, workshop, or consultation business based on what you know.

- Are there any current trends or markets you're interested in learning about that could become a business opportunity?

  Explore industries like sustainability, wellness, or e-commerce.

- What assets do you have that you could rent or sell?

  Think about property, vehicles, or even unused space for storage.

- How can you leverage social media or an online platform to create income streams?

  Social media allows you to reach a wide audience. From affiliate marketing to selling products, what could you use it for?

> "We don't save money to have more money. We save money to invest it and create freedom in our lives"
>
> Debbie Kempen

Chapter 5: Protect Your Credit Score

"Be patient and persistent!
Rebuilding takes time."

Debbie Kempen

One of the many things I learned the hard way from my divorce is that people aren't who they say they are. When the conversation about divorce first came up in my marriage, we agreed to be civil about it and do it on our own, so as to not accrue a ton of lawyer fees. It sounded good in theory, but what he meant was that I should sign off on whatever he wanted.

I went to the courthouse and picked up a big stack of divorce paperwork to fill out. I started to feel uneasy as we started filling out the child custody portion of it. He said he wanted me to write down that he would have them every other week. Except if he wanted to go hunting. I could have them when he was out hunting. Oh, and fishing. I could have them when he was fishing. It became clear to me that he was trying to avoid having to pay child support. He had told me a few years prior, in an oddly random way that if I ever left him, he would quit his job, and I wouldn't get a penny in child support.

Despite living together for 10 years, he had already been an absent father, so I wasn't surprised that he was choosing his own personal hobbies over his children. I felt like he was trying to take advantage of me when I was in a very vulnerable state, so I decided to get a professional's opinion on how to handle the divorce. When he realized I was stalling on signing the paperwork, he became furious.

I had been a stay-at-home mom for the last ten years. No career, no job, no money to my name. Fortunately, or rather unfortunately, a friend of mine had gone through a similar situation a few years before me. She told me to get $20 cash back every couple of trips to the grocery store and to hide it for when I'm ready to leave. It felt so wrong to do this, but I'm so glad I did. She also told me to order a secret container to store it in. I ordered a candle online with a secret compartment in the bottom of it and had it shipped to my parents' house. It has a can built into it with a screw off lid. I managed to save close to $1,000 this way.

We had a long history of abuse- physical, emotional, verbal and financial. When I reflect on the age-old question, "Why did you stay so long?" I am reminded of the fear I felt at the thought of our children being solely in his custody 50% of the time. As a stay-at-home mom I had 100% influence in my children's lives. He was rarely home anyway. When he was home he was staying up late, drinking. He would sleep most of the day away. As my oldest daughter got older I became more concerned about the example I am setting for her. If I am ok with living with a man like this, she might do the same in her future.

We left in a hurry after another one of his violent rages. He drained our bank accounts. I filed a protective order, and he was ordered to leave our home by law enforcement. After spending a few days with my parents, I tried to move back into our home, but it didn't feel safe there. The protective order did little to ease my fear.

I moved into a house closer to my parents. The rent was more than what I could comfortably afford by myself. We both ended up with lawyers and were in and out of court for 1 ½ years. After the first 6 months my ex's lawyer stopped representing him. My lawyer was convinced that my ex was dragging out our hearings to drain me financially. I would agree.

The final day in court finally arrived. I pleaded with the judge that my ex-husband be required to refinance whichever properties are awarded to him because I knew he would stop making mortgage payments to hurt my credit score. I was fully aware of the evil this man was capable of. When we received the final divorce decree, none of that was included.

Low and behold, as soon as he was awarded two of the investment properties, he stopped making mortgage payments. I received phone calls from the banks every single day for 18 months telling me that I'm late on my payments. I felt so hopeless, knowing that the properties legally don't belong to me, but are affecting my credit report. Meanwhile, he was collecting over $5,000 in rent every month *and* avoiding child support. That's a total of

$90,000 that he collected without having to suffer any consequences.

I requested another hearing with the judge. The judge told me that if I can pay what is owed on the properties, he would award them to me. It was way too much money at that point. I don't understand why it isn't standard procedure to refinance properties after divorce.

Along with foreclosures I also had a credit card closed on me. We had autopay set up from our joint account. That account was drained of its funds. I was making payments from a separate account I had. I called the credit card company to ask for a credit increase, and they said it was closed. What? Why? I was actively making payments on it still. They said the monthly autopay from the other account was triggering NSF, Non sufficient funds, charges which automatically warrants the card to be closed. When I attempted to re-open it they had to run my credit as if I was opening a new card. I was turned down because at this point I already had a few months of missed payments from the mortgages my ex husband wasn't paying.

This was the part of my life where I learned the painful lesson that there will be unpleasant things that happen that are out of my control. I cannot control the behavior of others. The phrase that got me through all of this was, "It is what it is". If I cannot control it, it is out of my hands and I don't need to be crying or stressing over it. It's easier said than done, but it actually gets easier with time. I have become very resilient to other people's bullshit. I accepted my fate that I would not be able to purchase anything that requires good credit for the next 10 years, when the foreclosures and closed credit card account would drop off of my credit report.

If you are struggling to recover from debt or things on your credit report after divorce, I recommend you call all the creditors in your name and let them know about your situation. Some creditors might be willing to negotiate the terms of your payments to offer temporary relief or restructure your payments. Put a freeze on your credit to make sure your ex isn't opening new accounts in your name. Monitor your credit report closely. You can access your credit report for free at www.annualcreditreport.org. It will not give you a score but it will show you what's on it. Create a budget. You might need to be on a tight budget for a bit as you recover.

Be patient and persistent! Rebuilding takes time. Try not to make emotional financial decisions. Give yourself grace and know that you *will* recover!

Chapter 6: Work With What You Have

"I will not let anyone make decisions about my life but me! I decide what I'm capable of. I decide my limits; and quite frankly, there are none."

Debbie Kempen

After a few years of simply surviving my daily life, I mustered up the courage to try again. No way was I going to let someone else control whether or not I keep investing! I started looking into alternative ways to invest that didn't require good credit or a lot of cash. There are many methods for this- wholesaling, sub-to, and owner finance to name a few. I ultimately decided to get a private loan and flip a small home. It seemed like the least risky option. I knew I would find a way to pay back the loan before the payment was due.

Wholesaling involves finding a property at a discounted price, getting it under contract, and then assigning that contract to another buyer, usually an investor, for a fee. Subject-to is a method where a buyer takes over the existing mortgage payments on a property while the loan remains in the seller's name. The buyer gains ownership, but the seller's name stays on the loan until it's paid off or refinanced. Owner financing is when the seller acts as the lender, allowing the buyer to make payments directly to them rather than obtaining a traditional mortgage from a bank.

I had a friend whose dad, and his coworkers, were interested in new ways of investing their money. I had a great neighborhood in mind that had smaller homes that needed some work. The average cost per home in that neighborhood was around $100,000-$150,000. I was hoping to receive a loan for $200,000 to make this flip happen.

I set up a meeting in a large conference room. It had a Shark Tank vibe to it, with 10 investors listening to my pitch. The pitch consisted of housing and economic data for that neighborhood- like the average cost of homes, increase in value over the years, and the growing population of medical health professionals moving to the area due to the hospital nearby. They took a few days to think about it and two of them decided they were willing to loan me $50,000 each for one year at 6% interest. "How can I invest $100,000 in real estate? Is that enough to do anything with?", I thought.

We wrote up a contract and met up at our local credit union to sign in front of a notary. After the three of us signed it, they transferred $100,000 into my account. I was SO nervous about signing for this loan, but I knew I would find a way to pay back the loan no matter what it took.

A few days later, I was going for a walk with my kids, and walked past this corner lot with a small for sale sign hanging in a tree. It was poorly advertised. I contacted the real estate agent from the sign and asked more questions. This lot had a mobile home on it in rough condition, so the seller was selling the lot for the value of the land only. There was a family living in the trailer. The asking price was $110,000. I started thinking I could offer $100,000 and continue renting the trailer to the family living there.

I called the real estate agent back and it didn't sound like they had any other offers on this listing, so I thought, "why not start low?" I submitted an offer for $90,000 and they accepted! I scheduled an appointment to view the inside of the mobile home and the family informed me that they had just put in an offer on another home. The new hurdle was to figure out how much work would need to be done to bring the mobile home to a marketable standard.

I hired a contractor and paid him $10,000 to make repairs, repaint, and put in new flooring. I started advertising it and showing it to people who were interested in renting. After a few showings I started to consider owner financing it to someone who could put down a decent down payment, after all I still had a $100,000 loan to repay in the next year. I started to advertise it for sale as an owner finance property.

A young family with extensive remodel and mobile home knowledge came and looked at it. They had a vision for this mobile home that exceeded mine. I sold them the mobile home for $50,000 at 10% interest with a $20,000 down payment. They rent the lot from me for

$600/month. Their total payment comes to $1248/month. We use an escrow company to handle the financials. They are a third party that holds and manages funds or documents during a real estate transaction. The buyer makes payments to them, just like a regular mortgage payment, and the escrow company deposits it into my account every month.

I was able to pay off the private loan within 18 months. I did ask for one extension. I financed my car, which had been paid off, to come up with the extra cash. The interest rate on the car payment was 2%, so it was an easy decision. My total expenses were $109,000. If I factor in the current cost of taxes, it will take a little over seven years to recoup the money I put into this property. After that, the land rent fee will be pure passive income.

The property is located in a central location, on a beautiful 1/4 acre lot, with a creek running in the backyard. It's zoned for a mobile home, single family home, or duplex. Should the family decide to move the trailer after they pay it off, I'll build a duplex on it and rent that out. The land is paid off and the initial investment will have been recouped by the owner financing of the trailer. I view this as free money. My only cost was learning the process and some of my time. If I build a duplex on this lot, I should be able to cash flow immediately. The tenants' rent will cover the mortgage, and I will start the process over again, building equity over time.

Throughout this process I did reach out to a real estate colleague for advice. A friend recommended that I reach out to him because he was well known for working with owner finance properties. He recommended a woman who works with the escrow company to draft up contracts and handle all of the legal stuff. Not knowing how to handle the paperwork was the most stressful part and working with her made it easy. This brings me back to the point of mentorship and the importance of surrounding yourself with successful people. You do not need to do this on your own. Successful people love helping others become successful. Networking helps you connect with other professionals who can make your life easier.

I'm very proud of this particular investment, not for the cash flow or increase in equity, but because I was able to do so much with so little. One of the reasons I'm so proud of this investment, is because it was my first real "fuck you" move. I will not let an abusive man decide my financial future! I will not let society tell me I cannot invest because I have his foreclosures on my credit report! I will not let anyone make decisions about my life but me! I decide what I'm capable of. I decide my limits; and quite frankly, there are none.

It would have been easy to fall into a victim mindset, blaming my ex-husband for the financial mess I was left to clean up, but being a victim doesn't get you anywhere — it keeps you stuck. Instead, I chose to focus on what I could do to move forward. Obstacles like a ruined credit score, limited resources, and the weight of rebuilding my life as a single mom were real, but they didn't have to define my future. Every challenge I faced became an opportunity to grow stronger and more resourceful. I learned that overcoming obstacles isn't about waiting for the perfect circumstances; it's about taking action despite imperfect ones. By refusing to see myself as a victim and committing to finding solutions, I turned what seemed like roadblocks into finding new ways toward financial freedom.

Life is full of obstacles, and while we don't always get to choose the challenges we face, we do get to choose how we respond to them. Overcoming obstacles starts with a mindset shift, from seeing difficulties as reasons to give up, to viewing them as opportunities to grow. I've faced plenty of setbacks in my life, from financial struggles to personal hardships, and each one tested my strength and resolve. But I realized that every obstacle was a chance to learn something new, develop resilience, and gain confidence in my ability to navigate uncertainty. It's not about avoiding problems; it's about finding a way through them. Whether it's rebuilding after loss or starting over with nothing, every challenge I overcame brought me closer to becoming the person I was meant to be. The key is to keep moving forward, even when the path ahead looks impossible.

You are not your past. You are not your circumstances. You can work hard to be happy, or you can struggle. The choice is yours. Life will always have its challenges, but you get to decide whether those challenges will break you or build you. You can choose to work hard, push through, and create a life of happiness and fulfillment, or you can choose to stay stuck in struggle. The difference is in your mindset and your willingness to take responsibility for your future. Happiness isn't something that just happens; it's something you build, day by day, through the choices you make and the actions you take. The power to change your life has always been in your hands.

Chapter 7: Investing with Confidence

"We have a limited time on earth to make impressions on our children, family and community that will instill positive changes and give us a legacy that lives on past our final breath. Why would you let ego and comfort get in the way of that?"

Debbie Kempen

What is confidence? Confidence is defined as the belief in one's abilities, skills, or judgments. It reflects trust in oneself to handle challenges, make decisions, and succeed in various situations. Confidence can be built through experience, preparation, and positive self-talk, and it influences how people approach tasks, interact socially, and manage setbacks.

One of the best things I've read and implemented about confidence was something I heard Brene Brown say on her podcast. She is a well-known research professor and author of social work, so she knows a thing or two about the topic. I had just been moved to a new position at work and it was really intimidating. Without getting into too much detail, if I fucked up at that job a lot of people could potentially lose their lives. The line of hers that I internally repeated to myself every single day until I no longer needed to was, "confidence is a choice." Sometimes you just have to suck up your feelings and get shit done.

In fact, I give myself internal pep talks on a regular basis. I refer to it as parenting myself. I have days where I am unmotivated and just want to lay around and doom scroll on my phone all day, eating junk food. On those days I have an internal conversation that sounds something like this, "You know you'll feel better after you go to the gym. You know you'll feel like shit tonight if all you did was lay around all day. You know you'll feel like crap tomorrow morning after poisoning your body with all this sugar. You know you'll feel better if you go for a walk. You know you'll have a better week if you meal prep today. Go to bed early so you don't feel like shit tomorrow"

Working a 9-5 with a pension plan, and medical benefits has been so ingrained into us as a path to success that many people don't consider other options, even if they're unhappy with their job. We take comfort in comfort. If you don't try something new you don't have to leave what's comfortable. If you don't try something new, you don't have to risk hurting your ego. If you don't hurt your ego, all is good in the world. Maybe your life is just comfortable enough to stay where you're at, but deep down inside of you, you know you were destined to do more- to be more. We all make choices in life. You chose to pick up this book because you want to change your life. Stop playing small.

Ego is such a powerful thing. It defines who we are as a person, or at least how we see ourselves in relation to the world. Ego refers to an individual's sense of self or personal identity; A person's self-esteem or self-importance, often with a negative connotation, implying arrogance or pride. According to Sigmund Freud, "the ego is the part of the personality that mediates between the id (instinctual desires), the superego (moral standards), and reality. It helps us make decisions that are realistic and socially appropriate." I no longer care about being "socially appropriate" in the context of how I choose to live my life. I do a lot of unconventional things for a woman, and it has gotten me so far in a short amount of time.

My life is like a book, and I am its author. With every life-changing event, good or bad, I am reminded that it is just another chapter in my book. This book is not being written out of thin air! These chapters don't just happen and get written *after the* events occur. These chapters can be planned out and written in advance. I have full control over what is being written. Sometimes, unpredictable events happen and we have to pivot and re-write. Every best-selling book has a rough draft.

We have a limited time on earth to make impressions on our children, family and community that will instill positive changes and give us a legacy that lives on past our final breath. Why would you let ego and comfort get in the way of that? You are the only person with the power to make the changes you need in your life to have financial freedom and peace. Which feeling is stronger? The feeling of comfort now, with the risk of regret later? Or discomfort and growth now to live a life with no regret later?

Our children are only children once. We have such a small window of opportunity to be their hero and to mold them into amazing people. One of my biggest motivators for investing in real estate has been to generate passive income so I can spend more time with my children. When I was in middle school my parents decided that their children no longer needed them. We could feed ourselves, bathe ourselves and fend for ourselves- so that's what we did. After many years in poverty, they decided it was time to focus on work and building up their retirement accounts. What I learned from that approach was this: The importance of investing and creating financial stability for the future, and that teenagers still need you. When I reflect on my happiest times in my childhood, it is the times when my parents were the most available and present. When we did the most activities together as a family.

Investing in real estate has given me the passive income I need to perfectly balance out the things that I deem most important in my life, my time and freedom. I am still in awe that I am able to live off my passive income and be available for my kids at 38 years old as a single mom. You really need to sit in silence and imagine this life for yourself for a few minutes. Truly feel the feelings. Imagine you accomplished this for yourself, and feel the pride. Imagine how peaceful and calm your life is from not having to stress about what your boss wants anymore. No more asking permission to take your kid to a doctor's appointment. Maybe you have a dream business you want to start. Perhaps even write a book. What would you do with the time given back to you from not having to work the job you don't love?

How do you build the confidence needed to start investing in real estate? You step outside of your comfort zone and just do it! Connect with other people doing it. Network with other investors. Talk to lenders. The more you know the easier it becomes. There comes a point, however, where you just need to start. You can start small. My mobile home venture was very profitable and it was my smallest transaction to date.

Lose the ego. Forget about what other people think about you. Redefine who you are to yourself. Talk to yourself the way you would talk to someone you love. We teach people how to think of us and treat us. Start talking about money and investing and you will attract like-minded people. Before you know it, people will be coming to you for advice and offering you great investment opportunities.

After my second abusive relationship, yes I had to learn that lesson twice, I decided to move to Germany with my children. As a single mother, by myself. I was initially intending on living off of my passive rental income and starting an online business but I was offered a job at a US military installation, so I accepted. I was planning on staying for one year but I ended up staying for three years. For the first two years I focused on traveling and spending time with my kids. It was a much-needed break from the rat race, even though I was still technically in it.

Though I worked full-time, the schedule still gave me a lot of opportunities to travel throughout Europe. I rediscovered my love for culture, amazing foods and new experiences. I found a whole tribe of women who enjoy traveling alone. I think a lot of that comes from the fact that we are always tending to other peoples' wants and desires. When we travel alone we can just go. We don't need to consult with anyone else and we can just go experience the new place. I found it so therapeutic to be alone in my thoughts, and observe the people and things surrounding me without someone interrupting. It's like meditation for those who can't sit still and quiet their mind.

After a while, I started getting the itch to invest in real estate internationally. I was initially looking into Portugal, because who wouldn't want to own a house in Portugal? Then I thought about the logistics. Why would I rent a house in Germany and pay someone else to manage a house in Portugal? Why not just buy a house in Germany? I had met so many Americans who only intended on staying in Germany for a few years and ended up staying for 15-20 years. They were renting the whole time and could have paid off a house already! What if I become one of those people that ends up staying for 20 years?

I started looking at houses for sale online. All of my coworkers strongly advised against it. As Americans working in Germany, we were only subject to US taxes. If the German government suspects that you plan on staying, they threaten to tax you as well. There was an ongoing lawsuit where an American was having to pay a large sum of German taxes. My kids were already going to German schools so the likelihood was stacking up. But when I want something bad enough, I make it happen! That is the woman I have become. Fuck the naysayers.

So I looked at a house. I fell in love with it, and I bought it. It was nerve-wracking, It was stressful, it was expensive, and it was so worth it! The process was completely different from that of the US. Some good, some bad. When I looked at the house, the seller and their entire family were present. I requested a second showing so I could bring a few trusted people with me to get their opinion, and to show the kids, of course. After walking through the house, we all sat down at the dinner table for coffee and pastries. That's right! The seller's whole family, my family and the real estate agent all sitting at the dinner table making negotiations over coffee at 8pm on a weeknight.

The most frustrating part was not knowing what my final expenses would actually be, because everything was split up. The taxes and insurance aren't rolled into an escrow account and tacked on to your monthly mortgage payment. I couldn't even find out what my property taxes would be because it supposedly violates the seller's privacy rights. Then there was the fact that the real estate agent was pressuring me to sign a contract before securing the loan. Um, no thank you! This contract was not contingent upon lending. I was not going to sign anything until my lender told me I could.

I didn't just love this house for me and my family. I saw all of the potential it had. The main two floors were beautifully remodeled in an Americanized way. It had a huge kitchen with a large refrigerator, and open floor design. All the modern comforts of home, but in a quaint little German town near the military base. The backyard has fruit trees for days that take turns blossoming in the spring and summer. I knew it would eventually become a rental property, and if I love this house, surely the next family will too.

Aside from being an amazing single family home, it had tons of potential to change things up. It's technically zoned as a duplex, with a separate entrance in the basement. The top floor and the main floor are separated by doors and a gorgeous, marble staircase. The basement could easily be converted into a mother-in-law suite, or separate apartment all together. If I add a kitchen to the top floor, it could be its own apartment as well. I figure if I decide to retire in Germany, I could have this beautiful house to live in, and rent out the basement apartment for additional income. It also has the potential to be converted into a triplex pretty easily.

I bought that house almost 20 years after buying my first house, having purchased many properties in between, and yet it felt like the first time all over again. As I was reviewing all of the documents on signing day, I remember feeling so overwhelmed and wishing I had a partner to help me verify that everything was correct. I was buying it with an additional lot, for a total of one acre, but it wasn't listed in the contract they prepared. I had to speak up and have them add it in there. The "Notar", the German equivalent to the title company, hand jammed it there. "Surely that's legit", I thought. Needless to say, I got through it on my own, everything worked out, and I absolutely *love* my home in Germany.

As for the naysayers? Well, they all started asking me how I did it, naturally. They wanted tips on which websites to use to shop for homes, which lender to go to, and which real estate agents to use. That lawsuit was settled, and it was deemed that the American did not owe the German government taxes after all. I'm so glad I listened to my gut and just went for it. It feels great to dance by the beat of my own drum.

I stepped out of my comfort zone, I tried something new, and it was so rewarding. I am now renting out that home to a wonderful family and generating passive income from it. It is a 20-year loan, so it will be paid off by the time I am 57. The interest rate is 3% lower than what US banks were offering at the time. Anytime I fly to Germany I can write off some of my travel expenses on my taxes as a business expense. Work smarter, not harder, right?

Use your resources! Most successful people love to talk about their success and help others achieve the same. Successful people aren't worried about competition. Talk to people who have done it. Use them as your blueprint. Ask them for recommendations. I have a ton of resources available on my website. We have a community of women investors waiting for you to join. We offer regular group and individual training if you need additional support to get started at www.debbiekempen.com.

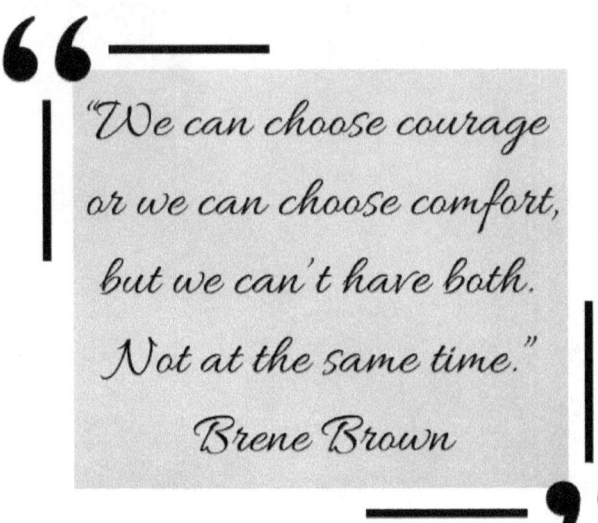

"We can choose courage or we can choose comfort, but we can't have both. Not at the same time."
Brene Brown

Chapter 8: The Blueprint

"Success in real estate isn't about perfection—it's about having a plan, taking action, and learning as you go."

Debbie Kempen

I bought my first house at 19 years old. It was a small starter home, in a community of zero-lot line townhomes, with an obnoxious Homeowners Association. Sadly, it's now one of the properties that only shows up on my credit report as a foreclosure. I didn't know what I was doing when I was buying a house at 19 years old. I had just gotten married, and my then husband deployed to Iraq shortly after. I went to a lender, who reviewed both of our credit scores and said that we didn't qualify due to his credit score. He handed me a printout of our credit reports, told me to call each creditor and pay them off.

Within a month I was back to tell the lender that I had called each creditor, negotiated a lower payoff amount and paid off each debt. He was shocked to see me back so soon, saying that most people take much longer to accomplish this type of task. He handed me a "90% letter" also known as a pre-approval letter, stating we were pre-approved for a home loan. When it was time to close on the townhome, there was still some question from the underwriter, the final approver of all loans, on whether we should qualify for this loan. My lender assured the underwriter we were good for the loan, and we closed shortly after.

I bought this house with a Power of Attorney. No one held my hand through the process. I didn't have a real estate agent helping me out. I didn't read any books on investing or scour the internet for information. I just did it because someone I trusted told me it was a good idea to do it. I have heard countless people tell me that they were given the same advice when they were younger, and they didn't do it and how much they regret it today. Those same people were still young enough to get started when they shared that with me, but somehow felt like the opportunity had passed them by. The truth is that it is never too late.

Buying real estate is likely the most expensive purchase you will make in your life. It requires a level of confidence and determination many people don't have. You can read every book available to you, watch every video, join all of the online communities and still not be prepared for buying your first real estate property. If you dig too deep into online resources, you'll find yourself overwhelmed. There are a hundred ways to get started but at the end of the day, you just have to start.

You are not the first person to want to invest and create wealth for you and your family. Stop overthinking the process. Overthinking can hold you back, leading to analysis paralysis, where you get stuck weighing too many options and never take action. Instead, make the decision to start and model your strategy after someone who has already achieved what you aspire to. Remember, it's perfectly fine to make mistakes and learn as you go. Every investor grows through experience, and each step forward, even imperfect, brings you closer to financial freedom. You *will* learn along the way!

Though that first townhouse is now just a memory and a ding on my credit report, I did buy another townhouse in the same neighborhood a year later. I do still own that one, and if you need more motivation to get started, here it is. I purchased this property for $205,000 with an FHA loan. I refinanced this property in 2014, which reset the 30 year loan, at a low interest rate. I have had tenants in this home for 16 of the last 17 years. It did not cash-flow very well. I made maybe $200/month on it, which is really just a cushion for repairs. It's not always about the cash flow though! I recently had this property appraised and it came in at $333,000.

Seventeen years might seem like a long time to turn some profit, but those 17 years were going to pass regardless. In those 17 years I have done very minimal work to maintain this rental. In those 17 years someone else has paid down that loan. In those 17 years this property has increased in value by 60%. That's $128,000! The loan is currently paid down to $135,000 and cash-flows approximately $750/month, but that's not what I'm celebrating. I'm most excited about the endless possibilities of what I can do with the equity.

With the equity of this property alone, I could take out a commercial loan, putting 20% down and buy a million-dollar property. It would mean making payments on two loans, and potentially not cash-flowing immediately, but as I stated previously, the current cash flow isn't the only money maker. It is easy to turn a property into a cash-flowing property over time. The real money maker is in having other people pay down your loan while your property increases in value.

If I wanted to cash-flow immediately, I could also sell the property and use the equity using a 1031 tax exchange. A 1031 tax exchange allows real estate investors to defer paying capital gains taxes by reinvesting the equity from the sale of one investment property into another "like-kind" property. To maximize the benefits, you have to reinvest all the equity from the original property into the new one. For example, if I were to sell this property for $333,000 with $128,000 in equity after paying off my mortgage, I would apply the full $128,000 toward the new property to defer taxes completely. This process requires strict adherence to timelines: you have to identify potential replacement properties within 45 days and close the purchase within 180 days.

Working with a qualified intermediary is a requirement, as they hold the sale proceeds to ensure compliance with IRS rules and help you avoid unnecessary tax liabilities. You can find more information on using a 1031 tax exchange on the IRS website at https://www.irs.gov.

That small starter home, in a community of zero-lot line townhomes, with the obnoxious Homeowner's Association, has the potential to grow into a million-dollar property. How amazing is that? It's proof that you don't need to start with a dream property to build real wealth. You can start small, and with time, patience, and market growth, it can transform into something incredibly valuable. This is the beauty of real estate—starting small doesn't mean you stay small. Each step builds on the one before it, and even the most humble beginnings can set you on the path to financial freedom. The important thing is to get in the game, because every property, no matter how small, holds potential.

In real estate investing, having a blueprint to follow is crucial because without a plan, it's easy to get overwhelmed by the countless decisions, market trends, and unexpected challenges. Analysis paralysis is real—if you spend too much time trying to figure out every little detail upfront, you might never take the first step. A blueprint simplifies the process, breaking big goals into manageable actions and helping you focus on what matters most, one step at a time. It gives you the confidence to move forward, knowing you have a clear direction, even if adjustments are needed along the way. Success in real estate isn't about perfection—it's about having a plan, taking action, and learning as you go.

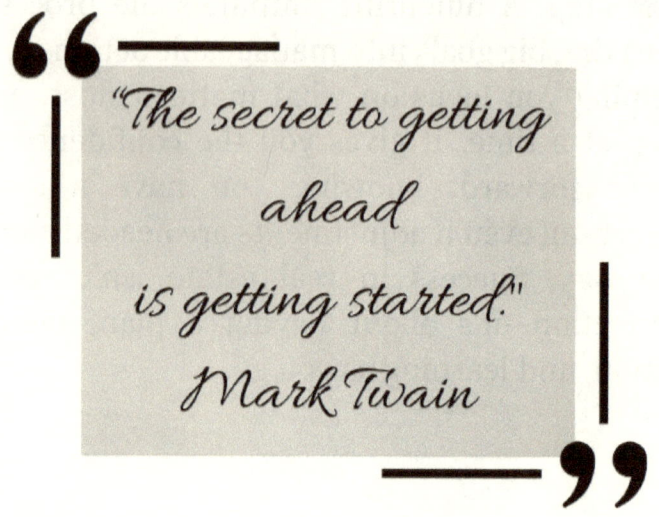

"The secret to getting ahead
is getting started."
Mark Twain

Chapter 9: Create a Legacy

"We're the pioneers- building wealth independently, becoming millionaires on our terms."

Debbie Kempen

You don't have to start investing in your 20s to be successful. In fact, there are many well-known examples of people who began their financial journeys later in life and still achieved incredible success. My dad, for instance, didn't become a landlord until he was in his 40s, yet today he's built an impressive real estate portfolio that has set him up for long-term financial stability. It's a clear reminder that it's never too late to get started in real estate or any form of investing. You can still reap the rewards, build wealth, and create the financial freedom you desire—whether you're 30, 40, or beyond. What matters is taking action and committing to the process.

No matter where you are in your financial journey, it's never too late to adjust your strategy and make progress toward your goals. If you haven't taken any steps to prepare for retirement yet, you'll likely need to adopt a more aggressive approach to catch up. The important thing is to recognize where you stand today, make a plan, and take action. You have the power to course-correct and still reach your goals, but it starts with being proactive and intentional about your financial future.

The average retirement age for a woman living in the United States is 62 years old, with our average life-span being 80 years old. Any property you purchase before the age of 50, with a 30-year mortgage, you are likely to see the day that it is mortgage free. Fortunately, that is not the only way we reap benefits from investing in real estate. You do not need to wait until you're in your 80's to celebrate real estate success; with careful planning and strategic investing, you can start reaping the rewards much earlier. Whether it's using the equity in your home to finance other investments, providing a steady cash flow through rental properties, or simply having a secure asset to pass on to future generations, the opportunities for celebrating your financial success can happen throughout your life. I have seen incredible growth in equity in my rental properties over the last ten years. The possibilities to leverage that equity are endless. Imagine what you could accomplish in 10 years if you started investing in real estate now.

Some ways to invest aggressively include house hacking, which I discussed in an earlier chapter, or the BRRRR Method. BRRRR stands for Buy, Rehab, Rent, Refinance, Repeat. I have a friend who bought a foreclosure for $275,000 and lived in it while remodeling it. He gutted the inside and rebuilt it from the ground up. He did most of the work himself using YouTube tutorials to guide him. It cost him $250,000 to remodel. When it was complete he had it appraised and refinanced. When it was time to start the next chapter in his life, he rented it out as a luxury short-term rental. After renting it out for a few years he decided to sell it. It sold for 1 million dollars! There was A LOT of sweat equity! The best part is, that because he lived in it for two of the last five years, he and his wife didn't have to pay capital gains taxes on

$500,000 of it. Where else can you make $500,000 tax free in two years?

I technically do not fall in the category of starting late, though I did overcome some major obstacles along the way, leaving me with no choice but to start over. I was 32 years old when my divorce was finalized. I did not have a retirement plan in place, nor did I have a career to lean on. I felt like I was so behind my peers! I knew I didn't want to work a job I hated until the age of 62 either! I was 34 when I worked up the courage to start investing in real estate again. This time with unconventional means, because that was my only choice (the trailer story). Looking back, I realize that 34 was not that old to be starting over.

I tried to look up some examples of women who started investing in real estate later than I did- say 40s or 50s. I could not find any. That's not to say that they don't exist, they just aren't publicized. A big reason for this is due to women in the United States only having been allowed to take out bank loans in the last 50 years. Let that sink in for a minute! Up until 50 years ago women could not take out loans without a male co-signer. The Equal Credit Opportunity Act (ECOA) of 1974 prohibited lenders from requiring male co-signers or treating women differently in any way during the loan process.

With that said, we are still the trailblazers of the feminist movement! We're pushing boundaries by boldly stepping into the world of investing—showing up to close transactions, break financial ceilings, and redefine what's possible. We're the pioneers- building wealth independently, becoming millionaires on our terms. We're the role models for the next generation. We are showing our daughters that they, too, can take charge of their financial future. The legacy we're creating now will be the stories of empowerment and resilience that inspire generations to come.

Chapter 10: House Hacking

I'm not sure when the term "house hacking" became a thing. It really irritated me when I first started hearing it on social media. I always just called it "investing in real estate". I'm pretty sure it's just a catchy term some social media influencer came up with. Regardless of whether or not I like the term, it was indeed one of my strategies in becoming a successful real estate investor and it's a great way to get started.

"House hacking" is a real estate strategy that allows individuals to live in a property while also generating income from it, effectively reducing or covering their housing expenses. A popular example is purchasing a multi-unit property (like a duplex, triplex, or fourplex), living in one of the units, and renting out the others. The rental income from the tenants helps to cover mortgage payments, property taxes, and other expenses.

When I bought my first fourplex, I was still married and already had three young kids, ages 1, 3, and 7. It seemed crazy, but we sold our single family house with a big yard, and moved to another city to live in a two bedroom, 1,000 sq ft unit. It was a new construction and was surrounded by dirt. The builder painted the walls and ceilings this yellowish-brown, baby poop color. The color of the walls and lack of natural lighting made the whole place look dim and drab. Considering this was in Alaska, where natural light is already scarce, it sucked.

Fitting a family of five into a small unit was not easy. We converted the single car garage into a storage unit. Anything we were not intending on needing in the next six months went in there. The girls shared a room with a homemade bunk bed, and built in shelving. The shelving was high off the ground for their toys. Keeping toys up high helped with keeping the place tidy, because they couldn't just dump out everything at once.

We could hear everything our upstairs neighbors were doing- Yes, *everything!* There were a lot of crazy things that happened that year. The life of a landlord is not a boring one! We had a young tenant upstairs who started inviting the wrong crowd over. One night, after one too many drinks, he decided to fire a shotgun at his uncle. No one was hit, but a bullet went through the apartment building and into the unit above ours. It hit a vase on a night stand. It happened to be a few feet above my daughter's bunk bed, where she places her head. He was evicted the next day. I hated living there, so we came up with a plan for the next big thing.

We financed the first 4plex using my ex-husband's VA loan (Veterans Affairs). If you are eligible for a VA loan, use it to buy a fourplex! It's the best way to maximize that benefit. If you don't have a VA loan available to you, you can still do this with an FHA loan. In both cases, the stipulation is that you "intend to owner occupy" the property. I have always been told to live in it for one year, but I've heard otherwise since then. Since I was also serving in the military, I also had a VA loan available to me. We found a property up the road from our fourplex and contacted a builder. We had a fourplex built with an owner's unit. We decided we wanted to be comfortable here for a while, so we made sure it had everything we wanted. The owner's unit has four bedrooms, 2.5 bathrooms, 2 car garage, 1800sq ft, and an acre lot. That's huge for a fourplex. Though we customized it to our needs, it has turned out to be very profitable as well. There are limited 4 bedroom rentals available, so it performs well. The rents received for that unit alone covers half of the mortgage payment for the whole building.

I rent that unit to families who end up staying long term. The less of a turnover a property has, the better. I have learned that having nicer rental properties attracts high quality tenants who take better care of it. Since most of my tenants stay long term, when they do move it's usually time to repaint and replace carpet, along with other minor repairs. These are expenses I like to put off as long as I can. Since I like having long term tenants, I treat this like a business and my job is to keep my customers happy. When they're happy, I'm happy. I'm not here to put shitty homes on the market and create stress for myself. I am providing a service and product I'm proud of. Fostering good relationships with my tenants has always been important to me and even created a few friendships.

One important thing to keep in mind as you're house hacking, is that your lender will want to know why you are buying multiple fourplexes using government-backed loans. Saying that you're building your real estate portfolio is not an option. You have to show that you need more space, or to move closer to work. In our case, we thought that having a bigger unit for our family was enough. Well, we didn't add any family members, so they didn't like that answer. We ended up saying it was closer to work and would cut down the commute, which was technically true, but not by much. So don't go buying a big, high-end fourplex if you plan on using government-backed loans back to back!

If you don't have a VA loan available to you, you can still house hack using your FHA loan. My suggestion is the same in maximizing your loan by purchasing a 4plex and owner occupying. If you have at least twenty percent equity in it, you can refinance it with a conventional loan without adding to the down payment and use your FHA loan again on another property. What does twenty percent equity mean? It means you have paid down twenty percent of the value of the home. Be mindful of interest rate changes, as it may not be a benefit to refinance. These things are always changing and it's best to talk to a mortgage lender to get current information

Find a trust-worthy lender you are comfortable with; someone who is extremely knowledgeable with the different types of loans. This can make a huge difference in how quickly and efficiently you build up your real estate portfolio. When you talk to a lender for the first time make sure they know you are wanting to buy a multifamily. When you apply for a loan for a multifamily they take the rental income into account when you are getting approved. Meaning, you might get approved for a $200,000 single family home, but if you tell them you are wanting to buy a 4plex your pre-approval number will be much higher. If you are wanting to do house hacking back-to-back, tell your lender up front. A good lender will give you tips on how to best make that happen.

THE EXCUSES

I have worked with and spoken to thousands of people, both men and women, about the benefits of real estate investing. One of the most common excuses I hear, especially now, is that...

Excuse #1

"It's not a good time to buy." At the writing of this book interest rates are the highest they have been in over twenty years. Mortgage rates significantly affect a buyer's purchasing power—the amount of home they can afford for a given monthly payment.

Higher rates, means higher payments: When mortgage rates rise, monthly payments increase for the same loan amount. This means a buyer would need a higher income or a larger budget to afford the same property. For example, a $400,000 loan at 3% interest might have a monthly payment of around $1,686, while the same loan at 7% could raise the payment to about $2,661. This reduces affordability, meaning buyers might need to lower their price range to keep monthly payments manageable.

Higher interest rates affect your DTI, Debt-to-Income Ratio (DTI), a key factor lenders use to approve loans. Higher rates increase monthly mortgage payments, which raises the DTI. If the DTI exceeds a lender's threshold (often around 43% of monthly income), the buyer may not qualify for as large of a loan or may need to look at lower-priced homes.

Rising mortgage rates may decrease your buying power, but I don't consider it a valid excuse when considering the purchase of an investment property and here's why. Interest rates were at a pretty comfortable number when I first started investing in real estate. They were comfortable for a long time. In 2020 interest rates were at an all-time low, but supply was also low, causing the cost of homes to sky-rocket. In the spring of 2022 interest rates started rising to five percent. This is when everyone started saying it's not a good time to buy because interest rates were too high. If you had purchased a 4plex in 2022 at 5% interest for $600,000 your monthly mortgage would have been $3,221/month, not including taxes and insurance (there are too many variables there to add to this example). Since 2022 interest rates have risen to 7%. That same loan is now $3,992/month. However, we're seeing record growth in equity in the United States right now, so the cost of that property has increased significantly in the last 2 years.

With an increase in interest rates and demand for housing, came increased rents. The cost of rent has gone up by 20% since 2020. Anyone who purchased a home prior to the rate increases is doing pretty well. Anyone buying rental properties now, should still be able to cover their mortgages with the rental income received. There was a time when buying a 4plex allowed for 3 units to cover the mortgage so the owner could live for free in the 4th unit, or rent it out and cash flow. At this point, I'm ok with a property just covering its own expenses. The rental income will pay down the loan, and I can always refinance to generate cash flow down the road. If you wait for interest rates to drop, the price of homes will have gone up too.

There are countless reasons people put off investing in real estate, even when they express genuine interest. I often hear individuals share their dreams of owning property or building wealth through real estate, only to follow up with a list of reasons why they can't or shouldn't take the leap. These reasons may appear practical on the surface, but they often mask something deeper: fear.

Fear of failure, fear of making the wrong decision, fear of financial loss, or even fear of stepping outside their comfort zone often lies at the root of these excuses. While it's natural to feel uncertain when exploring something new, allowing fear to dictate decisions can prevent people from pursuing opportunities that could transform their lives. Recognizing these excuses for what they are, the result of fear rather than genuine obstacles, is the first step toward overcoming them and moving closer to financial freedom.

Excuse #2

"I don't know how to get started." That's ok! We all have to start somewhere. We aren't born knowing this stuff. There are so many resources available to you and this book is a great start. Start with visiting a lender to find out what you are approved for. A good lender will give you some tips on what to do to reach your goals. Visit www.debbiekempen.com or connect with us on social media, if you want more detailed help with your investing journey.

Excuse #3

"I don't have good credit." I've had people tell me this and after I suggested they meet with a lender they found out that it wasn't true. They ended up buying a beautiful home with a huge yard to raise their babies in. This was shortly before interest rates started increasing. I'm sure they are thankful to have bought it when they did. You do not need perfect credit to qualify for a home loan. The only way to truly know is to talk to a lender. If you do not qualify for any amount, you can still go the private lender route, like I did for the mobile home.

Excuse #4

"I don't have enough for the down payment." How much money could you save up if your future depended on it? You don't need to give up your health or happiness to invest, but there may be some other areas where you can cut costs to save for a down payment. Short term sacrifices for long term gain might be necessary. Have you checked if you're eligible for any grants? Do you have any friends or family members who would be willing to lend you money for a down payment? You might be surprised by how little you need to get started.

Some loans require as little as 1% of the purchase price as a down payment.

Excuse #5

"My spouse doesn't have a job." I'm a single mom with three kids to take care of with sole financial responsibility. I have purchased two properties since that conversation. Meanwhile, interest rates and the cost of homes have gone up again. Is it true that they couldn't buy a property on one income? No. They made a good living. If your income is slim, start small. I understand that not everyone is excited to jump on the real estate band wagon, and that's ok, but don't blame your spouse!

Excuse #6

"I don't know how to be a landlord." Neither did I when I first got started at 19 years old. If a 19 year-old can do it, so can you. The first most important thing to do is to find a good rental contract template. All you need to do is fill in the blanks with the tenant's names, dates and have them sign it. You can get a copy of a template, along with other resources for beginners at www.debbiekempen.com. You might also want to consider having one drafted up by a local lawyer, as laws vary by state. Each state and country has their own set of landlord/tenant laws. You should be able to find them pretty easily. I make it a point to review them every single time I make a change (i.e. increase rent, post an eviction notice). If your budget allows, you could also hire a property manager. They generally charge 6%-10% of the rents each month, plus half of the month's rent when they need to find a new tenant. I have used property managers for the past two years, and am happy with my decision to do so.

Excuse #7

"I don't know how to fix things." Again, neither do I. Owning a rental property does not have a prerequisite of also being a handy-man. Is it helpful? Yes. Is it necessary? No. Networking with people in your community who have skilled trades is just as beneficial. Find a trust-worthy handyman who can be your go-to guy for repairs. If something exceeds their expertise they will let you know and you can hire a specialist.

Chapter 11: Why Real Estate?

There are hundreds of ways to invest your money and create wealth. Why do I keep going back to real estate? First and foremost, it's what I know and what I have grown to love. Don't fix what ain't broken! I've seen how fast I can make my money grow through real estate and I'm addicted.

When I invest in real estate, I physically own something. I can see it, I can touch it, and my name is on the deed. I can drive past it with my kids and say "I own this, and someday it will be yours." If I'm ever in a tight spot, I can always go back to living in my fourplex. It provides me the security of knowing I can always go home and have a place to live.

I have opportunities to give back to the community, whether it be by creating jobs, or providing housing for families. I once gave a single mom leaving an abusive relationship a place to live when no one else would. She had zero credit and half of her income wasn't on her paystubs because she was paid tips. Her employer was offering her a grant to help her out in her situation, but she needed a landlord to write them a letter, which I gladly did. She was a great tenant for 5 years.

Real estate investing provides some of the best tax advantages available. One benefit is depreciation, which allows investors to deduct a portion of the property's value each year as a non-cash expense, reducing taxable income. Mortgage interest is also tax-deductible, lowering the financial burden for those leveraging loans to purchase properties. Using a 1031 exchange, investors can defer paying taxes on profits from property sales by reinvesting in similar properties. Real estate investors can also deduct expenses like property management fees, maintenance costs, and even travel expenses related to managing or improving properties, so buy in places you like to travel to ;)

Rental income earned in the United States is considered to be earned in the United States. This means that if I decide to retire abroad I may not be taxed on the rental income I earn in the U.S. by that country. This depends on the tax laws of that specific country and any tax treaties it has with the United States. As a U.S. citizen you are required to report and pay taxes on your worldwide income, including rental income from properties in the United States, regardless of where you live. The U.S. allows you to claim a tax credit for income taxes paid to the foreign country on the same income. Many countries have tax treaties with the United States to avoid double taxation. For example, if I decide to retire in Germany I would be taxed on my rental income by the United States. Per the U.S.-Germany tax treaty I would also file taxes in Germany but I would not pay taxes on that income. This is a huge benefit as the United States taxes less than Germany. This is not the case for stocks and bonds. They would be taxed as personal gains at the German rate. If you are considering moving abroad, you should speak with tax consultants in both countries before finalizing your decision. The way you are taxed could make a huge difference in your quality of life.

One of my new favorite things about real estate is having the opportunity to pay my kids for the work they do on my rental properties. They have spent a few summers now mowing lawns for me. When I pay them for work completed, I can put it into their Roth IRA.

Imagine your kids having a generous amount of money saved up in their Roth IRA accounts before they even become adults. If you don't know, an IRA is an Individual Retirement Account, which is a type of retirement savings account that allows individuals to contribute post-tax income, meaning the money you deposit has already been taxed. The key benefit is that qualified withdrawals in retirement, including both contributions and any investment growth, are tax-free. Roth IRAs are especially advantageous for those who expect to be in a higher tax bracket in retirement or who want to minimize their taxable income later in life.

Here's a list of expenses that rental property owners can deduct on their taxes. Always consult a tax professional to ensure compliance with IRS guidelines and to maximize deductions based on your situation. By keeping detailed records and receipts, you can make sure you're claiming all eligible deductions while staying prepared for any potential audits.

- Property Management Fees
- Repairs and Maintenance Costs
  - Plumbing or electrical repairs
  - Painting
  - Appliance repairs or replacements
- Cleaning and Landscaping Services
- Utilities (if paid by the owner)
  - Water
  - Gas
  - Electricity
  - Trash removal
  - Sewer
- Mortgage Interest
- Property Taxes
- Landlord Insurance (e.g., hazard, liability, or flood insurance)
- Depreciation of Property (spread over 27.5 years for residential properties)
- Depreciation of Furniture and Appliances (for furnished rentals)
- Legal Fees (e.g., lease agreements, evictions)
- Accounting and Tax Preparation Fees
- Real Estate Investment Software or Tools
- Advertising Costs
  - Online listings

- - Signs
  - Photography
- Mileage for Property-Related Trips (e.g., showing the property, maintenance trips)
- Airfare, Lodging, and Meals for Out-of-Town Property Management
- Office Supplies
  - Paper
  - Printer ink
  - Filing cabinets
- Home Office Deduction (if you manage your properties from home)
- Internet and Phone Costs (portion used for property management)
- Tenant Screening Fees
- Eviction Costs
- Energy Efficiency Upgrades (may also qualify for additional tax credits)
- HOA Fees
- Pest Control
- Security Services or Systems

Chapter 12:
The End is Only the Beginning

*"Every day is a new opportunity
to create the life you want."*

Debbie Kempen

When I first started considering divorce more seriously, I was really concerned with statistics. Children who come from "broken homes" are more likely to be teen parents, end up in jail, have bad grades, have mental health issues, and end up in poverty. No way did I want that for my kids!

I have spent the last seven years as a single mom determined to break statistics. My kids do not come from a broken home. They *would* have if I had stayed with their dad. They do not suffer from a lack of love or stability. We will not suffer financially. They will not go to jail or end up pregnant at 16. We are a family that is whole and complete. We are healthy, mentally and physically. We are breaking stereotypes and setting aside excuses. We do not play victim to our circumstances. We will succeed because that is the only future we see for ourselves. If you want it bad enough, you WILL make it happen!

We really do have control of our lives. Every decision you have made in the past has gotten you to where you are today; good or bad. Accept responsibility for your actions that have gotten you in your current situation. Forgive yourself for the ones that didn't yield a good result. You cannot live your life in regret. Learn from your mistakes and move on.

Every day is a new opportunity to create the life you want. We've gotten so used to telling ourselves we're too busy when we think about the things we need to do to get ahead. The reality is, we make time for what is important to us. If you are not prioritizing financial freedom, what are you prioritizing? Financial freedom is important so you can better tend to the other high priorities. With financial freedom, you can get your time back! With financial freedom, you can spend more time with the people you care about. With financial freedom, you can take care of yourself; physically, mentally, and spiritually. Money does not buy you happiness, but it can buy you the freedom to create happiness!

Here I am, 38 years old. I am a survivor of domestic violence. I am a single mom of three smart, beautiful, charismatic kids. You would not know what our past entailed by where we are today. Seven years ago I thought my world was ending. Today I live in a beautiful home with a pool near the beach. I have the freedom to work when I want to work, if at all. A friend once asked me if I think I'll ever retire. My first thought was, "Hell Yeah! I'm retiring young!" but I thought about it for a second and said," No...I plan on doing work I love. Work that I don't want to retire from" I love investing in real estate and I love helping people. Why would I want to retire from that?

Investing in real estate has given me my time back. I have the privilege of driving my kids to school every morning, taking them to activities, and making them dinner without feeling stressed out. I have the time to take care of myself by going to the gym every day, baking my own sourdough bread, and laying out in the sun when I feel like I'm short on vitamin D. I can call up my friend and invite her over for lunch so we can dream up bigger dreams for ourselves, knowing damn well we'll make it happen, because that's the type of women we are. I have the time to fulfill my promise to help women create financial independence in their lives.

In some ways I feel like I have come full circle. I was a stay-at-home mom all those years, just to come back around and be a stay-at-home mom again, but this time it's different. This time it feels safe. I am safe to have my own ideas, dreams, and hobbies. I know I will always be safe financially. I have the freedom to do as I please. My home no longer holds space for negative energy.

Money doesn't buy happiness, but it buys me healthcare for when my children are sick. Money buys me vacations with my kids to create a lifetime of memories. Money buys me services that make my life easier, thus giving my kids a happier mom. Money buys me healthier food options and a gym membership. Money buys me a home I feel safe in, and in the best school district. Money doesn't buy happiness, but it sure as hell buys me the things that bring me peace and joy.

Money buys me freedom. The freedom to be present for my kids, freedom to dream bigger, and freedom to create a life we love without limits. I didn't get here by luck or by waiting for someone to save me. I got here because I refused to let my circumstances define me. I didn't settle for less, and I didn't let fear or doubt stop me. I chose to believe in myself and, more importantly, in the future I could build for my family. No matter where you are right now, you have that same power. You can break free from anything holding you back, rewrite your story, and build a life filled with meaning, purpose, and abundance. It's never too late to start, and it's never too late to dream a new dream. If I can do it, so can you. The life you want is on the other side of hard work, courage, and consistency.

If you were hoping for more technical stuff, or checklists, don't worry, I have you covered. Go to www.debbiekempen.com to find what you are looking for. If you feel like something is missing, send us an e-mail and we'll see if we can add it to our resource library. We would love to hear your success stories! Join our community and share tips so we can help each other grow. Leave a book review if you found this book helpful.

"*Success is a very intricate balance between pushing yourself into discomfort, while also listening to your intuition. Knowing the difference is hard.*"

Debbie Kempen

BONUS CHAPTER:
The Technical Stuff

HOW TO BE A
LANDLORD

Being a landlord is just managing people. If you have managed people at work, or children at home, you can be a landlord. Don't overthink it and trust yourself to find great tenants that will treat you with mutual respect. Go into this without fear and you'll be fine. Rest assured, mistakes will be made and people will fuck up, but that is life! You will learn from it and grow from it. Besides, it makes for great stories to tell.

I started my landlord "apprenticeship" when I was 14 years old. My dad had a few rental properties while still working his regular full-time job. My dad, being the frugal man that he is, was the last person on the planet to get a cell phone. He would advertise listings for vacancies online and list the landline for people to call. People called all the time. My siblings and I were expected to answer and had a list of questions to ask potential tenants. We had a blank piece of printer paper with hand drawn columns and categories listed on the top. We took down name, phone number, whether or not they had pets, and kids, and how soon they were wanting to move in.

When my dad came home from work, he would listen to all of his voicemails, and add their information to this sheet of paper. He would go line by line and call everyone back to schedule appointments for a showing. One tip he always mentioned to me was to judge a person by how clean their car is. He says the condition of their car is an indicator as to how clean they will keep your rental property. I personally don't go by this, because my car does not reflect the cleanliness of my home most days.

I've developed my own strategies through trial and error and will share them with you here. I am a huge fan of great marketing, while also not exaggerating what I have to offer. I love using professional photos of rental units and post them, along with a thorough description of what I am offering. I include a few sentences describing the layout of the home and the community it is in. I share how many bedrooms, bathrooms and garages it has. I am very clear in my advertising as to what my tenant criteria and expectations are. There are many websites you can post to. I post to Facebook Marketplace, in Facebook housing and sales groups, AHRN (If you are near a military installation), and MLS.

In recent years I have stepped away from conducting individual showing appointments. I have had too many people waste my time by not showing up. Now I host open houses and give prospective tenants staggered time frames to show up. I might have 10 people show up at 1pm, another 10 at 1:30, and 10 more at 2:00. Out of thirty people I might have 5 show up, and the staggered times work out nicely. If there is more than one family there at the same time it puts a little extra pressure on people to make a decision and fill out an application.

The application process is easy. I use mysmartmove.com which is run by Transunion. The tenant creates an account with them and answers all of the questions listed. They make a payment and the website runs their credit and background check. Both parties, the potential tenant and myself, receive a copy of both.

How do you know which prospective tenant is best? I try not to waste people's time or money. Since the application costs money, I try to get to know people as best as I can in the short amount of time I have at the showing. It's like a pre-screening. I do not expect tenants to have perfect credit. In fact, I don't even have a minimum credit score that I require. I look at a tenants credit history to try to gauge how likely they are to default on rent. If they have bad credit due to medical expenses or student loans but they pay their bills on time every month, they're good. If their income is $5000/month, rent is $2000/month, their monthly credit card bills are $2,000/month, they have 5 mouths to feed and still need to cover utilities, the answer is going to be no.

Always review your state's tenant/landlord laws! Do not put any discriminatory verbiage in your listings. It's against the law! Most state laws reflect those of federal laws. The Fair Housing Act (FHA), enacted in 1968 and officially known as Title VIII of the Civil Rights

Act, is a U.S. federal law designed to protect individuals from discrimination in housing-related activities. The law was originally passed in response to widespread racial discrimination and segregation in housing, especially following the civil rights movements of the 1960s. It was expanded in 1988 to add protections for people with disabilities and families with children.

Key Provisions of the Fair Housing Act:

The Fair Housing Act prohibits discrimination based on:

- Race
- Color
- National origin
- Religion
- Sex
- Familial status (protecting families with children)
- Disability

This means that landlords, real estate agents, mortgage lenders, and other housing-related entities cannot deny or restrict housing or treat individuals differently based on these characteristics.

The Act covers a wide range of housing-related activities, including:

– Renting and Leasing: Landlords cannot refuse to rent or unfairly charge based on a person's protected class.

Once you find a suitable tenant, send them your contract and ask them to fill it out. You can also print out two copies and fill it out in person. Make sure you leave a copy with your tenant. On the day of move-in conduct an initial walk-through. This is where you document any damages to the property. You will reference this document when they move out as you conduct a final walk-through. These protect both you and the tenant.

The day you hand your new tenant the keys you should also be collecting the security deposit and first months' rent. The security deposit is usually equivalent to one month of rent. The security deposit is a form of safety for you in case your tenant moves out and leaves things damaged or filthy on their way out. If you are taking a higher risk, you can charge a higher security deposit. For example: bad credit, no credit, criminal past, excessive pets, ect...

HOW DO YOU ASSESS IF A RENTAL PROPERTY IS A GOOD PURCHASE?

I've been hearing a lot about the 1% rule recently. The 1% rule suggests that a property's monthly rental income should be at least 1% of the purchase price. For example, a property purchased for $200,000 should ideally generate $2,000 in monthly rent. This rule provides a quick check for whether a property might be profitable, though it may vary by market. I personally don't use any special equations in determining whether or not a property is worth buying or not. I find that a property's investment potential is dependent on too many circumstances. I have purchased properties that would have failed the 1% rule that cash flow like crazy right now.

I don't like to overcomplicate things. If a property is located in a growing area, with a strong rental market and the mortgage is less than the incoming rent I say it's a suitable investment. If it needs work- great! Put a little sweat equity in it and charge more in rent for renovated units to create more cash-flow.

ABOUT THE AUTHOR

Debbie's journey is one of resilience, growth, and determination. Growing up in both Germany and Alaska, she experienced a diverse childhood that shaped her into a well-rounded person with a global perspective. Her love for hiking and travel reflects her adventurous spirit and appreciation for life's beauty.

With over 20 years of real estate investing experience, she has developed a deep understanding of building financial stability and wealth through smart investment strategies. However, her journey was not without challenges. After enduring a 10-year abusive marriage that brought significant financial setbacks, Debbie rebuilt her life with courage and tenacity, emerging stronger than ever.

Her experiences have fueled her passion for helping other women find financial freedom and independence. Through her personal story and real estate expertise, Debbie inspires women to take control of their financial futures, proving that it's never too late to start over and thrive.

SUMMARY

Single Mom Millionaire is a powerful and inspiring guide for women looking to take control of their financial future through real estate investing. Written by Debbie, a single mom of three with over 20 years of experience in real estate, this book combines personal stories of resilience and success with practical, actionable advice.

From overcoming a decade of financial setbacks after an abusive marriage to building wealth one property at a time, Debbie proves it's never too late to rewrite your story. Whether you're starting from scratch or looking to scale, Single Mom Millionaire will equip you with the tools, strategies, and mindset shifts needed to achieve financial freedom.

Packed with relatable examples and motivational insights, this book is perfect for women ready to turn their dreams into reality, no matter their age, background, or current circumstances. If you've ever thought, "I can't do it," this book will show you exactly why—and how—you can.

Let Single Mom Millionaire be your roadmap to financial independence and lasting wealth.

ACKNOWLEDGEMENTS & GRATITUDE

First and foremost, I want to thank my dad. Your wisdom, guidance, and unshakable belief in the power of real estate have been the foundation of so many of my successes. You taught me not just about properties and investments but also about resilience and striving for a better life. Your desire to provide your children with opportunities beyond what you had has shaped who I am today. You've also been a steady and positive male role model for my children, and I'm endlessly grateful for the love and stability you've provided in their lives.

Mom, thank you for instilling in me the profound understanding that nothing in life is more important than family. Your unwavering love and guidance have shown me the immeasurable value of being present for the people who matter most. You've taught me that success is not just about achievements or milestones but about the moments we create with the ones we love.

Michael, your unwavering faith in me has been a constant source of strength. Thank you for always believing in me, even when I doubted myself. Your encouragement to follow my dreams has meant more to me than words can express.

To my incredible kids—you are my "why." You are the reason I wake up every day with purpose and push myself to achieve more than I ever thought possible. I want nothing more than to give you a childhood filled with joy, adventure, and love. Watching you grow into such remarkable people fills my heart with pride. You are my greatest joy and the inspiration behind everything I do.

Alexis, you are proof that when we talk about what we want in life we are connected to like-minded people who help us grow. I knew you were my people when you said you want to own a $2million house someday. Everyone else laughed, thinking you were kidding. I knew better. I look forward to the many ideas we come up with to invest together. Stay ambitious, stay fearless, and never let anyone dim your dreams.

Shelly, thank you for being my mentor as I navigated the challenges of divorce and single motherhood. Your wisdom and listening ear got me through some tough times that no one else around me would have been able to relate to.

Mirav, meeting you came at exactly the right time. Your positivity, enthusiasm, and guidance as a writing coach were instrumental in turning my dream into a reality. For years, I told myself, "Someday, I'll write a book." With your encouragement, "someday" became "now." You pushed me to believe in my voice and my story, and for that, I am grateful.

To everyone who has been a part of this journey—whether through kind words, shared knowledge, or a listening ear — thank you. This book is the result of your encouragement, support, and belief in me. I couldn't have done it without you.

THANK YOU + CONTACT ME

Thank you for being a part of a growing community of women who are choosing personal growth and financial freedom.

Connect with us on-line at www.debbiekempen.com

SINGLE MOM MILLIONAIRE